# TRUE FRIENDS

## The Story of God and Abraham

By Rev. Darlene James

Illustrated by Joel Ray Pellerin

Rev. date: 04/04/2013

To order additional copies of this book, contact:
Xlibris Corporation
1-888-795-4274
www.Xlibris.com
Orders@Xlibris.com

# Dedication

This book is dedicated to the memory of my mother, Carrie Short, who laid a solid foundation for her children's spiritual development by the life that she lived even unto her death. She emulated for my brother, Reginald Warren, and I what a special relationship with God looked like. This is dedicated to the members of Zion Baptist Church in Welcome, Maryland, who played a major part in the foundational years of my spiritual development. This is also dedicated to my son (Mario Green), grandchildren, nieces, nephews, and extended family as they navigate their lives and relationship with God. The dedication extends to the teachers, parents, and children who seek to have a clearer understanding of their relationship with God through Jesus Christ.

# Preface

Many young people attend Sunday school week after week and hear the stories of the Bible. However, seldom does time provide the opportunity for them to react with understanding to the text, nor does the principle become an active part of their lives. This interactive story will provide the opportunity for children to interact, participate in the activities throughout the text, and reinforce their understanding.

# Acknowledgments

Thanks to my many friends and supporters who have been a part of bringing this work to fruition. Readers included Rev. Karen D. Harrison, Rev. Janet Habersham, Rev. Dr. Carrington Carter, Rev. Dr. Lois Poag Ray, Margaret Smith Perkins, and Pam Sherbia. I am grateful to the host of Sunday school workers and Bible study students who have shared their support during the years. I especially want to thank my husband, Benjamin James Jr., for his patience and encouragement.

We all like to have friends. Some friends are more special than others. Think about your best friends. What are their names? Why do you like them? Today, I want to share a story with you about two very special friends.

God found a man living in a country called Ur. This man's name was Abram. His name meant "exalted father." God told him to gather all his family and possessions and travel to a place where he would show him. Abram did not know where this place would be. Just imagine what would happen if your parents came home and said that you were going to a new place but they couldn't tell you where or anything about it. You would probably feel a little afraid or anxious. Abram had some concerns about this journey. But because Abram trusted God, he finally did as God told him.

One time, he passed through another king's territory. He was afraid that the king would kill him to get his wife, whose name was Sarai. He did something that he should not have

done. Abram lied to the king. Because Sarai was very pretty, he told the king that she was his sister instead of his wife. Have you ever told a lie because you were afraid? God was not pleased about the situation. The king took Sarai to be one of his wives because he believed Abram.

5

Many bad things began to happen in the kingdom. When the king found out that Abram had lied, he was disappointed in him, and he was very angry. He made Abram gather all his things and leave his kingdom. Abram had trusted God enough to follow his directions. Why couldn't he trust God to save his life? Have you ever been hurt by someone who told you something that was not true?

God asked Abram to do many things that he did not understand, and yet he was obedient. He made some promises to him because Abram had shown great faith in God. Faith is trusting without knowing or seeing what will happen or how it will happen.

He told Abram that he would make his name great in all the world. He would make him the father of a great nation. He would bless those who blessed him and curse those who cursed him. Every family on the earth would be blessed because of his obedience.

He promised to give the land Canaan to Abram's descendants as a place for them to live. Abram's descendants would be his children, grandchildren, great-grandchildren, great-great-grandchildren, and all the generations after that. This seemed strange to Abram because he was eighty-six years old and did not have any children.

As a part of the promise, God changed his name from Abram to Abraham, which means "father of many nations." There would be so many of them that their numbers would be like the number of pieces of sand on the seashore or equal to the number of stars in the sky.

He told him that many kings would come from him and that the new land of Canaan would always belong to his descendants.

But Abraham had no children!

One of the hardest things for people to do is wait for something that seems impossible to happen. Have you ever asked for something and had to wait? Sarai decided that she would help God out, and she told Abraham that she had a plan.

At last God promised Abraham a son by Sarai. He also changed Sarai's name to Sarah, which means "princess." She would become the "mother of many nations." The Lord promised Abraham that Sarah would have a child by the next year even though he was ninety-nine and she was ninety years old. She laughed when she heard about the plan.

Sarai's plan was to have Abraham have a child by her slave girl, and then she would count the child as her own. Abraham followed her plan instead of God's plan. Hagar had a child, and his name was Ishmael. Ishmael was not the child of promise. His birth seemed like a good idea, but it caused trouble for Abraham. Have you ever done something that seemed like a good idea and then it turned out not to work?

But God was faithful, and their son, Isaac, was born. Because Sarah did not like having Ishmael in her house with Isaac, she asked Abraham to send him and his mother away. Abraham was upset, but God made a promise to Abraham that he would take care of Ishmael. Since he trusted God, he decided to send them away.

Isaac grew up, and one day, God asked Abraham to do something very hard. He told Abraham to take his son, Isaac, up to the mountain and sacrifice him. In those days, people sacrificed animals to God. The blood of the animals symbolized the sins of the people being covered so that God could forgive them for their disobedience. Yes, they killed animals, but we don't do that anymore because God had a better plan that would later be revealed through his son, Jesus.

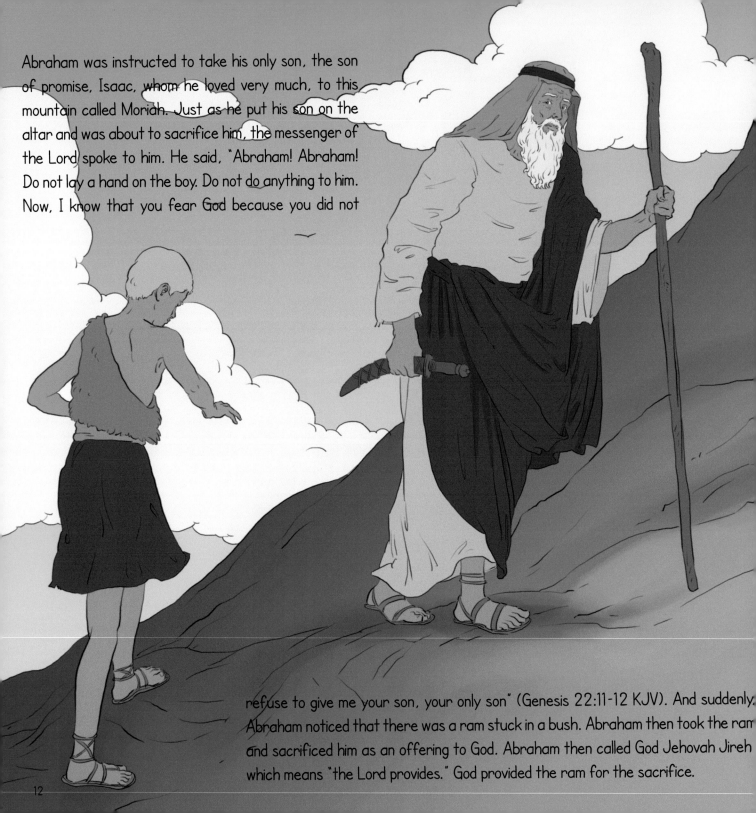

Abraham was instructed to take his only son, the son of promise, Isaac, whom he loved very much, to this mountain called Moriah. Just as he put his son on the altar and was about to sacrifice him, the messenger of the Lord spoke to him. He said, "Abraham! Abraham! Do not lay a hand on the boy. Do not do anything to him. Now, I know that you fear God because you did not

refuse to give me your son, your only son" (Genesis 22:11-12 KJV). And suddenly, Abraham noticed that there was a ram stuck in a bush. Abraham then took the ram and sacrificed him as an offering to God. Abraham then called God Jehovah Jireh which means "the Lord provides." God provided the ram for the sacrifice.

Abraham believed God, and that faith was regarded by God to be his approval of Abraham. So Abraham was called God's friend (James 2:23 KJV).

Just as God was Abraham's friend, God also wants to be your friend. Abraham had a son that was promised, and through his son, Isaac, the promises to Abraham would be fulfilled.

Abraham wanted to sacrifice his son because he wanted God to know how much he really loved him and he believed God's promise that there would be descendents that would come from Isaac. Even though he did not understand how God would do this, he was willing to hold on to the promise. I hope that you have enjoyed this story about Abraham and God in the book of Genesis chapters 12 through 24.

God is your friend too. God also had a son of promise whose name was Jesus. He is called the only begotten son of God. He was both human like us and divine like God. This may sound strange to us, but it is one of the many mysteries of God. Just like Abraham didn't always understand and had to accept things by faith, we must also do the same.

God sent his son, Jesus, to die on a cross. His blood covered the sins of Abraham's descendants. We are Abraham's descendants, not by birth, but by our faith in God. Abraham would later be called the father of faith (Hebrews 11).

Why is this important? It is important because we must believe that Jesus really is the son of God and that God raised him from the dead so that we could become members of the family of God. Just as in the case of Abraham with Isaac, God provided the sacrifice.

If we believe that Jesus is the son of God and the fact that God raised him from the dead, then we also receive a promise from God. The promise to us is that we will have a chance to live forever with God in heaven. We will not only be a friend of Jesus but also a friend of God. Jesus said in John 12:44, "He that believeth on me, believeth not on me, but on him that sent me."

As a friend of God, you will obey his commandments and listen to God when he speaks to you. God says, "If you love me, you will keep my commandments." We obey our parents because we love them and because God tells us to obey them. Likewise, we live by and follow his rules.

Your friend wants to talk with you today. He wants to protect you and take care of you, not only today, but every day, if you are willing to listen.

Now that we have finished reading this story, we are going to do some things to help you remember this story. It is more than just a story. Here are five activities that you can do to help you remember this story.

# Appendix

The following activities will help you share your understanding of the story of the friendship between God and Abraham.

## Activity No. 1

If you have never said to God that you want to be his friend, here is a way to do it. This is not the only way but just a suggestion. Simply tell him, "Father God, I believe that Jesus died for my sins and that you raised him from the dead. You said if I believed, then I could receive, and so I receive my salvation and membership into the family of God."

# Activity No. 2

Find twenty words from the story hidden in the word search.

| God | Jesus | Isaac | Abram |
|-----|-------|-------|-------|
| Abraham | Ur | Sarah | Sarai |
| protect | friend | faith | trust |
| disappointed | Moriah | bless | sacrifice |
| provide | mysteries | promise | begotten |

| j | k | m | e | n | i | s | a | b | g | n | m | e | G | o | d |
|---|---|---|---|---|---|---|---|---|---|---|---|---|---|---|---|
| p | r | o | t | e | c | t | m | n | t | a | b | r | a | m | m |
| w | i | l | s | a | c | r | i | f | i | c | e | u | c | e | k |
| s | a | r | a | h | o | m | e | u | r | k | f | a | i | t | h |
| f | r | i | e | n | d | n | l | h | t | r | u | s | t | i | t |
| p | j | e | s | u | s | k | p | r | o | v | i | d | e | s | z |
| d | i | s | a | p | p | o | i | n | t | e | d | f | j | a | x |
| m | y | s | t | e | r | i | e | s | w | q | s | a | r | a | i |
| d | a | b | r | a | h | a | m | v | g | f | v | m | b | c | e |
| z | m | o | r | i | a | h | u | y | s | r | b | I | e | s | s |
| p | r | o | m | i | s | e | c | b | e | g | o | t | t | e | n |

What was your score? _____ /20

## Activity No. 3

Answer the questions to show how well you read or listened.

1. Who was the man that God found in Ur?

2. What was the first thing God wanted him to do?

3. How was he able to do this strange thing?

4. What character trait did Abram show that caused the king to be disappointed and angry with him?

5. What happened to the king and his people because he believed Abram's lie?

6. Name two promises God made to Abraham?

7. Who was the child of promise in the story?

8. How did the people during Abraham's time get their sins forgiven?

9. How do you become a friend of God?

10. What must you do with God's laws/commandments if you are his friend?

## Activity No. 4

Pretend that you are the king. Write a letter to Abram from the king. Let him know how disappointed you are in him. Let him know how it affected your land. Tell him how it will affect your relationship with God.

## Activity No. 5

Share the story with a friend or family member and tell them how they can become a friend of God. Share with them the prayer that is found in activity no. 1.

*True Friends: The Story of Abraham and God* is an interactive book that allows the reader the opportunity to gain knowledge about the special relationship between God and Abraham. This story will help them relate it to their own lives. They will obtain an understanding of what it means to have a special relationship with God. For just as God loved Abraham enough to make promises, he also loves and continues making promises to us. His promise is one that we can always count on, even though we can't figure out how, when, where, and why. The activities will help us understand more and more about God and his relationship with humankind. It is an opportunity for children to understand what it means to have a special relationship with God.

Copyedited by May Vinece T. Sienes
Reviewed by Leia Albiar

Printed in the United States
by Baker & Taylor Publisher Services